Liberty

An Illustrated History of America's Favorite Statue

Kevin Woyce
Photographs by the Author

A Delafield Press Book
2015

Kevin Woyce

"Colossal statuary does not consist simply in making an enormous statue. It ought to produce an emotion in the breast of the spectator, not because of its volume, but because its size is in keeping with the idea that it interprets, and with the place which it ought to occupy."

—Frederic Auguste Bartholdi, 1885

Liberty Enlightening the World (1886).

Table of Contents

Frederic Auguste Bartholdi, 1880. (Napoleon Sarony)

Chapter One

Bartholdi

Frederic Auguste Bartholdi spent more than 15 years working on the Statue of Liberty.

He was born in Colmar, a French village in the hills of Alsace, in 1834. His father, Jean Charles, died two years later, and his mother, Charlotte, never remarried. She raised Frederic and his older brother, Charles, in Paris, but always brought them home to Colmar for vacations. Their house is now the Bartholdi Museum.

Both boys studied painting, but neither made a career of it. Charles became a lawyer. Frederic studied architecture with Eugene Emmanuel Viollet-le-Duc, author of the *Dictionary of French Architecture*, and then turned to sculpture. He completed his first major work—a statue of General Jean Rapp—in 1855. (Like Bartholdi, Rapp was born in Colmar. He fought alongside Napoleon in Egypt and Russia, and defended France's eastern border during the Emperor's brief return to power in 1815.) The statue is still in Colmar, along with several other Bartholdi sculptures.

In October of 1855, Bartholdi joined a group of French artists and sculptors for a nine-month tour of Egypt and the Near East. Visiting Giza, they saw the

Pyramids and the Great Sphinx. (Four thousand years after it was carved, the lion's body was buried to its shoulders in the desert sand. Archaeologists would not finish uncovering it until 1936.) At Luxor, Bartholdi gazed up at the twin Colossi of Memnon— 64-foot quartzite statues of the Pharaoh Amunhotep II. In his 1885 memoir, he wrote, "those marvelous ruins ... had a very considerable effect upon my taste for sculpture."

Edouard de Laboulaye taught history and law at the college of France. Though he never visited the United States, he was a great admirer of all things American. In 1849, he taught the first French course on the United States' Constitution. He had to drop the course two years later, when Louis Napoleon declared himself "Emperor Napoleon III." Though limited to teaching ancient history and the history of law, Laboulaye never lost his interest in our nation. In 1855, he began writing a three-volume *Political History of the United States*. Throughout the American Civil War, he served as president of the French Anti-Slavery Society, and wrote and spoke in defense of the Union (in the early days of the war, many Europeans favored the Confederacy). In the 1860s, he began translating the writings of Benjamin Franklin for French readers. (Franklin, who convinced the French to support the American Revolution, was one of Laboulaye's heroes.)

In the spring of 1865, Laboulaye invited a group of friends to dinner at his home near Versailles.

Bartholdi later described most of the guests as "men eminent in politics and letters." They discussed the recent Union victory, the end of slavery in the United States, and the assassination of Abraham Lincoln, whom they all admired. They also talked of the long friendship between the United States and France, which Laboulaye believed was "sustained with common aspirations. The Frenchman who fought in the United States spilled their blood for the principles that they hoped to see prevail in France and in the world."

Toward the end of the evening, Laboulaye suggested that "a monument ... be built in America as a memorial to their independence." He hoped it could "be built by united effort ... a common work of both nations." He did not say what sort of monument he had in mind, and may not have given the matter much thought; nobody in France would be building a monument to freedom so long as Napoleon III ruled the Second Empire.

Bartholdi left Laboulaye's house that evening with a commission for a bust of the scholar, which he completed the following year. More importantly, the dream of an American monument "remained fixed in [his] memory."

"Napoleon le Petit," as Victor Hugo called the Emperor, was Bonaparte's nephew, elected president of the short-lived Second Republic in December, 1848. In a short book published in exile and smuggled into France, Hugo dismissed Louis as a

"vulgar, commonplace personage" who "lies as other men breathe." Regarding comparisons to the first Napoleon, he wrote: "There is ... a slight difference between conquering an empire and pilfering it."

In Paris, 1867 was the year of the *Exposition Universelle*. Between April first and October 31, more than nine million people visited the industrial and artistic displays in the *Champ de Mars*. The park's main building was an iron and glass *Palais* a mile around, built by railroad engineer Gustave Eiffel. There were also two lighthouses, and a full-size replica of a Gothic cathedral. Mark Twain was fascinated by the native costumes worn by foreign visitors, Jules Verne by the electrical displays.

One of the fair's most popular exhibits was a detailed model of the soon-to-be-completed Suez Maritime Canal. When Egypt's ruler, Khedive Ismail Pasha, visited the fair, Bartholdi suggested marking the canal's entrance with an enormous statue. Two years later, at the canal's opening, he gave the Khedive a sketch titled *Egypt Carrying the Light to Asia*. Egypt was depicted as a peasant woman holding up a lantern. The monument would have risen 132 feet above the desert sand, the 48-foot woman (86 feet to the top of her raised lantern) standing on a 46-foot stone pedestal. Put a light in the lantern, or in her crown, and the statue could double as a lighthouse.

Pasha kept the sketch, but dismissed the project as too expensive to build.

Prussian Chancellor Otto von Bismarck maneuvered Napoleon III into declaring war on Germany in July, 1870. The Germans captured the Emperor in September, and then surrounded Paris. By January, the city's population was reduced to eating horses, pets, and zoo animals. Three weeks of nightly bombings convinced the leaders of the new Third Republic—just established following Napoleon's capture—to surrender, on January 28, 1871.

When the war began, Bartholdi enlisted in the French National Guard. At Bordeaux, he arranged transportation for "arms and munitions" delivered by American ships. Talking with the ships' officers, he learned that, despite scattered pro-German demonstrations, most Americans sympathized with France.

Discharged in 1871 with the rank of major, Bartholdi found himself a man without a home. The Treaty of Frankfurt, signed in May of 1871, gave Alsace and Lorraine to Germany; France would not regain these provinces until the end of the First World War. "At Paris," Bartholdi wrote, "the Commune was in power and civil war was raging." (The Paris Commune was a radical government that seized power after the Third Republic surrendered to Germany. The civil war that toppled it lasted three months, claiming 33,000 lives.)

Kevin Woyce

Lion of Belfort (1880).

Frederic Bartholdi dedicated this red sandstone lion, 72 feet long and 36 feet high, "To the Defenders of Belfort, 1870-71." (The city of Belfort remained French territory after the Franco-Prussian War because 15,000 men, many of whom were not even soldiers, defended it for 103 days against 40,000 invaders.) The hammered copper version of the lion that stands in Paris was made from Bartholdi's 1878 plaster model, a third the size of the sandstone monument.

Canadian sculptor George William Hill made a small granite copy of the lion for Montreal in 1897.

Picture: French postcard, "BELFORT—LE LION," published in Belfort around 1910.

Visiting Laboulaye at Versailles, Bartholdi said he was considering visiting the United States. Newly elected to the National Assembly, and hard at work on the Republic's new constitution, Laboulaye wrote a letter of introduction and arranged the trip.

He also gave Bartholdi a mission:

"Go to see that country ... Propose to our friends over there to make with us a monument, a common work, in remembrance of the ancient friendship of France and the United States."

Did you know?

Bartholdi's architecture teacher, Viollet-le-Duc, restored many of France's medieval buildings. Unlike modern restorers, he often added elements that were not part of the original design; his restoration of Notre Dame Cathedral added a third tower to the Paris landmark.

Colmar dedicated a 39-foot copy of the Statue of Liberty on July 4, 2004—the hundredth anniversary of Bartholdi's death.

Trinity Church, New York (1848).

Chapter Two

Designing Liberty

Bartholdi crossed the Atlantic on the steamship *Pereire*, arriving in New York Harbor on June 21. "The view when one arrives at New York is marvelous," he wrote. "It is, indeed, the New World."

Today, it is difficult to imagine New York as he must have seen it. Trinity Church was the city's tallest building. Completed in 1848, its 286-foot steeple overlooks the narrow entrance to Wall Street. Nearby, in the East River, workers were digging foundations for the Brooklyn Bridge. The tower on the Brooklyn side of the river was completed first, in 1875.

Bartholdi spent five months touring the United States, sketching and painting and looking for the perfect place to build the monument. With Laboulaye's letter of introduction, he visited President Grant at his summer home in Long Branch, New Jersey; Civil War generals Meade and Sheridan; Peter Cooper, who built America's first steam locomotive in 1830, and then established Cooper Union as a free university in 1859; and the poet Henry Wadsworth Longfellow, author of *Paul Revere's Ride* and the *Song of Hiawatha*. Bartholdi returned to France encouraged by their reactions, and certain that the monument should stand on one of the small islands in

Kevin Woyce

New York Harbor. "The Statue," he wrote in 1885, "was born for this place."

Naturally, Bartholdi saw the monument as a colossal statue. With Edouard de Laboulaye, he agreed on a subject: *Liberty Enlightening the World*. They made Liberty a Roman goddess, because our word "Liberty" is derived from the Latin *Libertas*. In the mythology of ancient Rome, Libertas was a goddess who represented both personal and political freedom. Worshipped first by freed slaves, she eventually had temples throughout Europe, and her profile stamped on Roman coins.

As a symbol of freedom, Libertas has long outlived the Roman Empire.

The French call her Marianne. In 1789, her image was stamped on medallions celebrating the storming of the Bastille prison, at the start of the French Revolution. Painter Eugene Delacroix imagined her leading an armed rabble during the July Revolution of 1830. Since 1999, her profile has been part of the French Republic's red, white, and blue logo.

The English call her Britannia, which was the Roman name for the islands in the first century A.D. Since Roman times, Britannia has been depicted as an armor-clad warrior goddess, armed with trident and shield. Her likeness has often appeared on British coins and stamps, and in 1953, she gave her name to Queen Elizabeth II's Royal Yacht. Decommissioned in 1997, her 412-foot *Britannia* is now a popular tourist attraction in Edinburgh.

In the 1700s, many Europeans still called the Americas "Columbia," in honor of Christopher Columbus. The name was also given to the first female symbol of the New World. Originally pictured as an Indian maiden in native regalia, Columbia had transformed into a Classical beauty in flowing white robes by the time the United States won their independence. Like Uncle Sam—and later the Statue of Liberty—she was a common figure on political posters and propaganda.

Columbia University is named after her. So is the capital of South Carolina and the federal District of Columbia—the "D.C." in "Washington, D.C." Since 1928, she has held the torch in the Columbia Pictures logo and been the "C" in "CBS," short for "Columbia Broadcasting System." She has also lent her name to ships, airplanes, and two spacecraft: the Apollo 11 Command Module that brought Neil Armstrong, "Buzz" Aldrin, and Michael Collins to the moon in July, 1969; and the Space Shuttle *Columbia*, which flew 28 missions between 1981 and 2003.

Before designing the Statue of Liberty, Bartholdi studied the colossal statuary of the ancient Egyptians, Assyrians, and Greeks. They taught him the importance of "great simplicity" and of choosing just the right location for a monument, so "the lines of the ground and the coloring of the background become his assistants in heightening the proper appearance of his work."

Kevin Woyce

Two of the Greek statues Bartholdi described in his memoir are counted among the Seven Wonders of the Ancient World: the Olympian Zeus (462 B.C.), and the Colossus of Rhodes (280 B.C.).

Phidias was Athens' most famous sculptor. After supervising the decoration of the Parthenon, he spent eight years at Olympia, carving a 40-foot statue of Zeus from sheets of ivory (for skin) and gold (for hair and clothing). In Athens, Phidias had used the same method, called *chryselephantine*, for a colossal statue of the goddess Athena, which stood for hundreds of years in the Parthenon. Both statues were concealed deep inside their temples, where only priests were allowed. Everyone else saw them from a distance, and then only when the priests opened the curtains that protected them from sun and storms.

Phidias' Zeus watched over the site of the ancient Olympic Games for almost 900 years, before disappearing early in the Fifth Century. According to legend, it perished in a fire after being moved to Constantinople. (A similar story is told of his statue of Athena, which disappeared around the same time.) Modern historians believe the statue was destroyed, along with its temple, when the Roman Empire converted to Christianity. Whatever its fate, archaeologists found no trace of Zeus when they excavated the temple's ruins in 1875.

Rhodes is the Mediterranean's easternmost island. For 56 years, its harbor entrance was marked by the Colossus, a 100-foot bronze statue of the sun god Apollo. Toppled by an earthquake in 224 B.C., the statue lay in ruins until 672, when it was sold for scrap. Roman historian Pliny the Elder wrote, "Few men can clasp the thumb in their arms, and the fingers are larger than most statues." Legend tells that the merchant who bought the old bronze needed 900 camels to cart it away!

The Colossus was hollow, and partly filled with stones for stability. It may have been used as a lighthouse, guiding ships into the harbor; if so, there had to have been ladders or stairs inside.

Old prints and engravings of the Colossus often show it standing with one foot on either side of the harbor entrance. "This legend," Bartholdi wrote, "whose origin is not older than the sixteenth century, has been exploded by archaeologists." His own research convinced him "that the placing of a statue of this kind in an upright position would be almost impossible."

Impossible or not, the "legend" has survived in the popular imagination. In her 1883 poem The New Colossus, *Emma Lazarus contrasted Liberty with "the brazen giant of Greek fame, with conquering limbs astride from land to land." The harbor-spanning statue has also appeared in books, video games, and movies—including Sergio Leone's 1961 directorial debut,* The Colossus of Rhodes, *in which the ancient wonder is used as a fortress.*

Bartholdi sculpted a four-foot clay model of the statue in 1874. After approving the design, Laboulaye gathered his wealthiest and most influential friends to form a fundraising organization they called the French-American Union. In keeping with Laboulaye's earliest ideas about the monument, the Union decided the building costs should be split among the French and the Americans: the French would pay for the statue; the Americans would build her a pedestal.

Underestimating the technical difficulties of building so large a statue, the Union expected the work to cost about $250,000. They began soliciting donations in September, 1875, and held an elaborate fundraising dinner that November. Entertainment included the new *Liberty Cantata*, written and conducted by Charles Gounod, composer of the operas *Faust* and *Romeo and Juliet*.

Left: This terracotta copy of Bartholdi's original clay model is displayed in the museum on Liberty Island.

Although one of France's largest metalworking firms, Japy Fréres, donated all the copper used in the statue, her cost eventually reached $400,000—more than eight million in 2011 dollars. To make up the difference, the Union sold lottery tickets and souvenirs, including 200 terracotta copies of Bartholdi's four-foot model, each one signed by the artist himself. (Bartholdi also helped raise money by publishing *Album du Bord*, a book of drawings he made while traveling to the United States aboard the steamship *L'Amerique* in May, 1876.)

Bartholdi built his next three models of wood covered with thin layers of plaster. The first was nine feet tall, the second more than 36 feet high, and the third full size: 151 feet (so big it had to be built in four sections). The dimensions of each enlargement were set by measuring every detail of the previous model (about 1500 points) in three dimensions, and then multiplying every number by four. Each model was more detailed than the last, allowing Bartholdi and his assistants to refine every detail before beginning construction.

Carpenters used the full-sized model to make more than 300 wooden molds of the statue's head, arms, robes, and feet. Workers at the Parisian metalworking firm of Gaget, Gauthier & Company then heated thin sheets of copper and hammered them into the molds to create the statue's skin. (Called *repoussé*, this method was chosen because Liberty would be too big to cast—or transport—in one piece.)

This wooden mold, used to make the toes on Liberty's left foot, is displayed at the Statue of Liberty museum.

As the hammered sheets were removed from their molds, stiff iron "ribs" were attached to their inside faces to hold them in shape. But even with the iron bands, the copper would not be self-supporting. Though Liberty is so big that her copper skin alone weighs more than 80 tons, this skin is only as thick as two pennies—about 3/32 of an inch. And if the statue was to stand in the middle of a harbor, Bartholdi needed to find a way not only to support all this weight, but to keep the thin copper sheets from blowing apart in heavy winds.

Two engineers worked on the problem. The first was Bartholdi's old architecture teacher, Eugene Viollet-le-Duc. Though known mostly for his work on historic buildings, Viollet-le-Duc was also one of the first architects to consider building with iron. His framework for the head was used, but his plan for stabilizing the statue—by dividing her interior into chambers that could be filled with sand, and then emptied one at a time for maintenance—was not.

Gustave Alexandre Eiffel came to the project after Viollet-le-Duc died in 1879. Since supervising the construction of the Saint-Jean railroad bridge at Bordeaux (1858-60), Eiffel had planned and built some of the world's most impressive bridges and aqueducts. (He had also collaborated on the design and construction of *Le Bon Marche*, the world's first iron and glass department store.)

The armature Eiffel designed for Bartholdi looks very much like a bridge support. Four iron uprights, connected by horizontal beams and strengthened by cross-bracing, form a central pylon 97 feet high; this structure bears the entire weight of the statue. Iron beams radiating from the pylon support an outer framework, shaped roughly like the statue. The iron "ribs" attached to the copper are then linked to this outer framework by hundreds of metal "springs," which allow Liberty to sway as much as three inches in heavy winds. (The torch, held up by an additional 40 feet of ironwork, moves up to five inches.) For stability, the pylon is anchored to two sets of beams built into the concrete and granite pedestal.

Kevin Woyce

Scale model of Eiffel's armature, at the Statue of Liberty Museum.

In 1889, Eiffel used a similar design to build what would remain the world's tallest tower until 1930, when New York's Chrysler Building was completed. Rising from the *Champ de Mars* in Paris, the Eiffel Tower was the centerpiece of the 1889 *Exposition Universelle*, celebrating the hundredth anniversary of the start of the French Revolution. Though it contains 18,000 pieces, held together by more than 2.5 million rivets, the thousand-foot tower was completed in little more than two years.

Many Parisians considered the tower ugly when it was completed, and looked forward to its scheduled demolition in 1909 (Eiffel held a 20-year lease, after which the tower became city property). After the Exposition closed, Eiffel demonstrated the tower's usefulness by taking wind measurements, studying weather patterns, and broadcasting radio signals. Today, it is the world's most popular monument, drawing seven million visitors a year.

Thomas Edison, who displayed his phonograph at the Exposition, visited the Eiffel Tower several times. Although he admired it, he predicted the United States would build a taller one for Chicago's 1893 World's Fair. (Instead of a tower, engineer George Washington Ferris built a huge observation wheel.)

"Must-See" attractions at the 1889 Exposition included the iron-and-glass Galerie des Machines ("Machinery Hall"), filled with the world's latest inventions; and Buffalo Bill Cody's Wild West Show, featuring sharpshooter Annie Oakley.

Kevin Woyce

The tablet Liberty holds in her left hand is 23 feet tall and 13 feet wide. The date in Roman numerals is July 4, 1776: the day the Declaration of Independence was signed in Philadelphia. When he returned to France after his 1871 trip to America, Bartholdi hoped to complete the statue for the hundredth anniversary of the signing: July 4, 1876. Political and financial troubles caused by the Franco-Prussian War delayed the start of fundraising efforts until the fall of 1875.

Early sketches showed Liberty holding broken chains in her left hand (they now lay at her feet). Replacing them with a tablet—one of the world's oldest symbols of Law—may have been Laboulaye's idea. At the College of France, he taught that freedom could not survive unless it was protected by a system of laws, such as the United States' Constitution.

Several smaller copies of the statue displayed in France have two dates on the tablet. The second is July 14, 1789: the day the French Revolution began with the storming of the Bastille prison. Like our own Independence Day, Bastille Day is an annual holiday celebrated with parades and fireworks.

The Brooklyn Bridge opened in 1883, three years before the Statue of Liberty, which can be seen from its walkway.

Did you know?

Visitors to Paris can see Bartholdi's 9-foot model of the Statue of Liberty at the *Museé des Arts et Métiers*, a museum of science, technology, and invention. Founded in 1794, and housed in a restored medieval priory, the *Museé* is home to Foucault's Pendulum, which was built in 1851 to prove that the earth rotates daily. Other exhibits include early airplanes, mechanical calculators, and 1980s supercomputers.

Bartholdi's widow donated the fragile wood and plaster model in 1907. More than a century later, art dealer Guillaume Duhamel contracted with the museum to scan the model and produce a dozen bronze castings. The first he gave to the museum, the others will be offered to collectors for a million dollars each.

Since October 28, 2012, three National Park Service webcams have been providing real time and panoramic views from Liberty's torch, which was closed to visitors in 1916.

Chapter Three

Building Liberty

Bartholdi did not try to build the statue all at once. The first part he completed was the right hand and torch, which he shipped to Philadelphia for the 1876 American Centennial Exposition. Visitors paid 50 cents each to climb ladders up through the arm and stand, a dozen at a time, on the balcony underneath the copper flame. The admission fees helped finance the statue's construction, and the display gave Americans their first glimpse of its size (the index finger is eight feet long!).

President Grant opened the Exposition on May 10. By the time it closed on November 10, more than 10 million people had visited the United States' first World's Fair. Popular exhibits included Alexander Graham Bell's first telephone, an early Remington typewriter, and the world's largest steam engine.

For Bartholdi, 1876 was a busy year. He visited New York in September, for the dedication of his statue *Lafayette Arriving in America* in Union Square, where it still stands today. A few days later, he made his first trip to Bedloe's Island, where he hoped to place the Statue of Liberty. He helped establish fundraising committees in New York, Philadelphia, and Boston, and on December 20, he married his

fiancée, Jeanne-Emilie, in Newport, Rhode Island. They returned to France after honeymooning at Niagara Falls.

Left: Liberty's right hand and torch, in Philadelphia for the 1876 American Centennial Exposition.

In addition to Liberty's right hand and torch, Bartholdi exhibited four bronze statues and a monumental fountain at the Centennial Exposition. Landscape architect Frederick Law Olmsted, who designed New York's Central Park, convinced Congress to purchase the fountain for the United States Botanic Garden, on the Mall in Washington, D.C. The fountain was moved to its present location— Bartholdi Park, on Independence Avenue—in 1933.

Built of cast iron covered with bronze, the Bartholdi Fountain is 30 feet tall and was originally lit by a dozen gas lamps. Each of the three nymphs is 11 feet tall.

Early 20th century postcard view of the Bartholdi Fountain, as it appeared when the U.S. Botanic Garden was located on the Mall in Washington, D.C.

Bartholdi's *Lafayette Arriving in America* (1875) in New York's Union Square Park.

Bartholdi sculpted two statues of the Marquis de Lafayette. The first was given to the city of New York by the French Fellowship Society in 1875 and dedicated on September 6, 1876—Lafayette's 119th birthday. Originally designed for Central Park, the statue was placed in Union Square at the request of the city's French citizens, who felt that Central Park's planners were taking too long to choose a location.

Newspaper publisher Joseph Pulitzer commissioned the second statue in 1888, as a gift to the people of France. Having already depicted Lafayette's arrival in America, Bartholdi now sculpted him meeting George Washington for the first time. He showed the statue in Paris in 1892, and then brought it to the Chicago World's Fair in '93. Since 1895, Lafayette and Washington has stood in Paris' Place des Etats-Unis ("United States Square").

Although critics on both sides of the Atlantic found fault with the statue, New York businessman Charles Broadway Rouss liked it enough to commission a copy. He donated the sculpture to the city, and it was dedicated on April 19, 1900, in a small Harlem park at the intersection of 114th Street and Manhattan and Morningside Avenues.

Lafayette was the orphaned son of a wealthy French officer who died fighting the British in the Seven Years' War (fought between 1756 and 1763, and known in the United States as the "French and Indian War"). Though he was just 19 when he bought a ship and sailed to America, the Continental Congress made him a major general.

Kevin Woyce

King Louis XVI of France was not so pleased. Louis had not yet decided to support the American Revolution, had forbidden Lafayette to sail, and ordered the young Marquis arrested when he returned to France in 1779. By the following year, however, the King had changed his mind, and sent Lafayette back to America—with the men and ships Washington needed to defeat Cornwallis in Virginia and win the war.

Lafayette returned to France in 1782. Though he believed in the ideals of the French Revolution—he helped compose the influential "Declaration of the Rights of Man and of the Citizen"—he soon found himself at odds with leaders who replaced the old monarchy with a rule of terror. During Napoleon's reign, he held no government positions and declined to serve in the army.

In 1824, Lafayette accepted President James Monroe's invitation to tour the United States. During the year-long trip, he visited all 24 states and paid his respects at George Washington's Mount Vernon tomb. Congress repaid the loans he made during the American Revolution with $200,000 and land in Florida.

When this equestrian statue of George Washington was dedicated in 1856, it stood in the street south of Union Square. The oldest sculpture owned by the New York City Parks Department, it was moved to its present location inside the park in 1930. Sculptor Henry Kirke Brown (1814-1886) depicted Washington returning to New York on "Evacuation Day," November 25, 1783—the day the British left after occupying the city since 1776. A copy was made in 1916, for the United States Military Academy at West Point.

New York had not had an equestrian statue since July 9, 1776, when a group of citizens melted down a lead statue of King George III to make musket balls for Washington's army.

After the Centennial Exposition closed in November, Liberty's right hand and torch were moved to New York's Madison Square. Located at the intersection of Fifth Avenue, Twenty Third Street, and Broadway, the former military parade ground was named after our fourth president, James Madison, in 1814. By 1877, when the torch arrived, Madison Square was one of New York's most popular parks, recently landscaped by the new Department of Public Parks and surrounded by some of the city's most fashionable neighborhoods. Although the park fell into disrepair in the last decades of the 20th century, the landscaping and monuments have since been restored, and are now cared for by the Madison Square Park Conservancy.

Intended to raise interest in the statue—and money for her pedestal—the torch remained in Madison Square until 1882, when it was shipped back to France. Eiffel's framework had been assembled behind the Gaget, Gauthier & Company workshop, where the copper skin was being hammered into shape.

The Flatiron Building (1902), one of New York's first skyscrapers, stands just south of Madison Square.

Levi Morton, United States Minister to France, had driven the first of 300,000 temporary rivets on October 24, 1881—the hundredth anniversary of the British surrender at Yorktown. By June, 1884, all 350 copper pieces were in place.

The French-American Union officially gave the statue to the United States on July 4, 1884. Ferdinand de Lesseps, architect of the Suez Canal, made the presentation (Lesseps had been elected president of the Union after Laboulaye died in 1883); Levi Morton accepted for the United States.

Lesseps became the chief promoter of a French-built Panama Canal in 1879. He underestimated the cost and the difficulty of the project, and the canal company declared bankruptcy ten years later, after collecting almost $400 million from investors.

Following his term as Minister to France, Levi Morton served as Benjamin Harrison's vice president (1889-93) and governor of New York (1895-96).

Bartholdi began disassembling the statue in January, 1885. As the temporary rivets were removed, first the copper skin and then the iron framework were packed into a total of 214 wooden crates. Loading the half-million-pound cargo of iron, wood and copper aboard the French frigate *Isere* took 17 days. Delayed by storms, Liberty arrived in New York Harbor on June 17, 1885. After all the crates were unloaded onto Bedloe's Island, where they would be stored until the pedestal was finished, *Isere* returned to France in July (her usual job was carrying supplies and soldiers to French colonies).

Did you know?

Although Bartholdi wanted Liberty to stand on Bedloe's Island, the decision was not his to make. When Congress voted in 1877 to accept the statue, and to provide her a home in New York Harbor, the War Department owned Bedloe's, Governor's, and Ellis Islands. The Army still maintained the forts on Governor's and Bedloe's, and the Navy was storing ammunition on Ellis. Since Ellis was too small for the proposed monument, Congress asked Commanding General William Tecumseh Sherman—the nation's highest ranking military officer since Grant was elected president in 1869—to choose between Governor's and Bedloe's.

After considering the strategic value of both islands—Governor's was larger and closer to Manhattan—Sherman suggested placing the statue where Bartholdi had always imagined her: in the center of the star-shaped fort on Bedloe's Island.

Kevin Woyce

The New York skyline, photographed from the walls of Fort Wood (1811) on Bedloe's Island.

Chapter Four

Islands

Liberty Island was known as Bedloe's Island until 1956, when the name was changed for the statue's seventieth birthday. The older name had been in use since the late 1600s, when the island belonged to Isaack Bedloo, a Dutch merchant and customs collector.

Bedloe's was one of a group of three small islands near the New Jersey shoreline (the other two were Ellis and Black Tom). Because they used to be surrounded by rich oyster beds, the Lenape Indians called them the "Oyster Islands." Ellis was later named after Samuel Ellis, who opened a sailors' tavern there in the 1700s. According to local legend, Black Tom got its name from an African American fisherman who once lived on the island.

The federal government acquired Bedloe's and Ellis Islands in the early 1800s, and fortified them in time for the War of 1812. Measuring less than three acres at high tide, Ellis was just large enough for a 20-gun battery, powder magazine, and barracks. On the larger Bedloe's Island, the War Department built an 11-pointed masonry fort, whose walls were 24 feet high and 20 feet thick at the base.

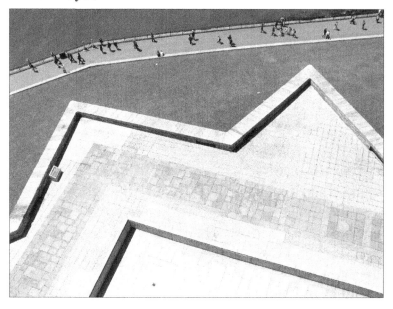

Two of Fort Wood's 11 points are visible in this view from the top of Liberty's pedestal. In case of attack, the points allowed the fort's garrison to defend the walls with a deadly crossfire.

Neither fort was ever tested in battle. During the War of 1812, their presence—as parts of a well-planned system of forts and batteries in and around New York Harbor—was enough to discourage a British attack on the city.

Both forts were named in 1814, after officers killed in the Battle of Lake Erie (August 15, 1814). "The Works on Bedloe's Island" became Fort Wood, and the Ellis Island battery became Fort Gibson. Colonel Eleazer Derby Wood graduated from West Point in 1806, supervised the construction of the forts on Governor's Island, and designed and built several forts on the shore of Lake Erie. Colonel James Gibson, who stands beside Wood in an 1840 painting of the battle (*Repulsion of the British at Fort Erie, 15th August, 1814,* by E.C. Watmough), graduated from West Point in 1808.

The Manhattan Indians called the harbor's largest island "Nut Island," for its stands of chestnut, oak, and hickory trees. The name survived among the Dutch, who bought the island in 1637, as "Nutten Island."

In 1664, a British fleet arrived to conquer New Amsterdam. Unhappy with reigning Dutch Governor Peter Stuyvesant, the city's residents surrendered without a fight, and the British claimed Nutten Island for the use of their Colonial Governors. Although the island has been popularly known as Governor's ever since, the name was not officially changed until 1784.

George Washington's army fortified the island with 40 cannons in the summer of 1776. On the night of August 29, the guns held off the British fleet long enough for the Americans to cross the East River from Long Island, where they had been defeated at Brooklyn Heights, to lower Manhattan. Abandoned a few days later, the island's defenses were manned by British soldiers until 1783.

The island's two stone forts were built in the early 1800s, to help defend New York from foreign attack. Fort Jay is a star-shaped masonry fort in the center of the island, Castle Williams a round sandstone battery on the northwest shore.

Castle Williams, completed in 1809, has a diameter of 210 feet. Its sandstone wall is 40 feet high and seven feet thick, and each of its three floors held 26 cannons.

Fort Jay was named for John Jay: president of the 1778-79 Continental Congress; our nation's first Chief Justice; and governor of New York from 1795-1801. Fort Williams was named after its designer, Colonel Jonathan Williams: a military engineer and the first superintendent of the United States Military Academy at West Point.

Improvements in naval artillery soon made masonry forts obsolete. During the Civil War, the Army used Forts Jay and Wood as recruiting stations, and housed Confederate prisoners in Castle Williams. By the 1870s, Bedloe's Island was used mostly for storage, and occasionally as a quarantine station.

Castle Williams, photographed from Manhattan's Battery Park.

The military history of Governor's Island ended in 1995, with the closing of the nation's largest Coast Guard base (the Coast Guard occupied Governor's Island in 1966, after the Army post closed).

President Clinton declared the island's forts a national monument in 2001. Two years later, the federal government sold the rest of the island (150 acres) to the people of New York. The city has since created the Trust for Governor's Island, to redevelop the old military base as a scenic park with a large historic district and a two-mile waterfront promenade.

New York Harbor, photographed from the top of the pedestal. In the foreground, a passenger ferry approaches Liberty Island. In the distance, the 1964 Verrazano-Narrows Bridge spans the harbor entrance. (The bridge is named for the Italian explorer Giovanni da Verrazano, who wrote the first known description of the harbor in 1524.)

The Staten Island Ferry has been part of the harbor scenery since 1817, when the Richmond Turnpike Company launched the steam-powered *Nautilus*. "Commodore" Cornelius Vanderbilt added the company to his steamship empire in 1838, and then sold it to the Staten Island Railroad in the 1860s. New York City took over the service in 1905, after a series of accidents, and has operated the ferries ever since.

In 1972, fares were increased for the first time since 1897—from five cents to 10! The ferries have been free to ride since 1997.

Chapter Five

Pedestal

Once her site was selected, Liberty needed a pedestal to stand on, and a foundation to raise it above the walls of Fort Wood. In 1877, an American Committee gathered to begin designing and raising money for these massive works.

Like the French-American Union, the American Committee was a group of wealthy and influential men; most lived in or around New York. Chairman William Evarts was a founding member of the New York Bar Association, and its first president. He had successfully defended President Andrew Johnson during his 1868 impeachment trial, and had just been named Secretary of State by President Rutherford B. Hayes (1877-81). Other members included poet and journalist William Cullen Bryant, who had been editing the powerful *New York Evening Post* for nearly 50 years (New York's Bryant Park is named after him); Edwin Noyes, former Ohio governor and newly appointed United States Minister to France; and John Taylor Johnston, former president of the Central Railroad of New Jersey, founder and first president of the Metropolitan Museum of Art. The New Jersey town of Butler is named after the

Committee's secretary, Richard Butler, who owned the town's biggest industry, the Butler Hard Rubber Company. As secretary, Butler maintained a long correspondence with Bartholdi, becoming the sculptor's closest American friend. Celebrating this friendship, the Statue of Liberty is featured on the Borough of Butler's Coat of Arms.

The American Committee is often criticized for moving slowly on the pedestal, and thereby delaying the statue's completion. They did not choose a design until 1884, and construction stalled several times due to a lack of funding.

They did, however, face challenges unknown to the French-American Union. When that group was formed, the statue had already been designed and approved.

The American Committee needed to design a pedestal massive enough to support the statue, but simple enough that it would not divert attention from Bartholdi's masterpiece. They also wanted to build it for around $125,000 (the final cost was twice that, or five million in 2011).

The Committee hired Richard Morris Hunt, one of America's most popular neoclassical architects, in December, 1881. He had designed mansions for New York's wealthiest families, and the 260-foot red-brick headquarters of the *New York Tribune*. Later works would include the Vanderbilts' North Carolina "Biltmore" estate; the Administration Building for Chicago's 1893 World's Fair; and New York's Metropolitan Museum of Art.

After submitting several designs which the Committee rejected, Hunt presented plans for a pedestal based on one of the Seven Wonders of the Ancient World. The Pharos of Alexandria was an Egyptian lighthouse, completed in 283 B.C. and used for more than a thousand years. Badly damaged by earthquakes, the ruins were torn down in 1346 to make room for a fortress. Fort Qait Bey—still standing, and one of Alexandria's most popular attractions—was built partly of stone salvaged from the Pharos. The Committee approved Hunt's design on July 31, 1884, but later requested that it be shortened and simplified. Hunt, who designed the pedestal for free—he received a thousand dollars for his efforts, but donated it all to the construction fund—approved the changes.

Masons laid the cornerstone on August 5, 1884. Only fifteen feet of the 89-foot pedestal were completed by the end of the year, when the American Committee ran out of money and halted construction.

Early work on the pedestal, and on its 62-foot concrete foundation, was paid for by donations from some of New York's wealthiest citizens. Steel baron Andrew Carnegie contributed, as did Rockefellers and Astors; showman and museum entrepreneur P.T. Barnum; and Cyrus Field, who laid the first transatlantic telegraph cable in 1866 (it took him attempts). An 1883 Art Exhibit, sponsored by the National Academy of Design, brought in another $14,000.

Kevin Woyce

But the Committee did not want the pedestal to be paid for by just a handful of millionaires. In France, people of every age and class gave money to build the statue. Why couldn't the same thing happen here in the United States?

The Committee faced several problems. First, many people around the country saw the statue as New York's monument, or as a lighthouse for New York Harbor; why should anyone but New Yorkers pay for it? Second, monuments were still a new idea in the United States, and not all that popular (the Washington Monument, begun in 1848, was not completed until 1885). And third? Some Americans were still suspicious of this "pagan goddess" the French wanted to send us. Building a monument to celebrate the Battle of Bunker Hill, or to honor the Father of Our Country, was one thing; "Liberty Enlightening the World" was another.

Newspaper editor Joseph Pulitzer made it his mission to change people's minds.

Born in 1847, Pulitzer was the son of a Budapest shopkeeper. He left Hungary at the age of 17 and rode with the First New York Cavalry during the closing months of the Civil War. After the war, he moved to St. Louis, Missouri, where he eventually found work reporting for the city's German-language newspaper, the *Westliche Post* (along with his native Hungarian, Pulitzer spoke German, French, and English). He bought the *Post* in 1872, and merged it with the *St. Louis Evening Dispatch* six years later.

Pulitzer bought the ailing *New York World* from financier Jay Gould in 1883. Under his direction, the *World* quickly became one of the city's most profitable and influential newspapers. Pulitzer courted the city's workers and new immigrants with crime stories and scandals, publicity stunts, cartoons, and outspoken editorials. But he also wrote about the things that mattered to them. He exposed corruption wherever he found it, criticized the monopolies and supported the unions.

When it seemed Liberty's pedestal would never be finished, Pulitzer took his readers to task. He reminded them who paid for the statue in France—ordinary people like themselves—and told them not to wait for the city's "millionaires" to pay for her pedestal. He then promised to print the name of every person who donated, no matter how much or how little anyone gave. Soon, the money was pouring in; by May, 1885, the American Committee had the $100,000 it needed to finish the pedestal. As work resumed on Bedloe's Island, Pulitzer kept his word to his readers. Though most donations were less than a dollar, he printed the names of all 120,000 people who responded to his pleas.

The pedestal was completed on April 22, 1886.

Hunt planned to build the entire pedestal of stone. To save time and money, the American Committee built it of reinforced concrete, with just an outer facing of granite from a Connecticut quarry. The 13 courses of rough granite at each corner represent our original 13 colonies.

The four square columns on each side of the pedestal suggest the Roman temples dedicated to the goddess Libertas, and the architecture of ancient Athens, where democracy was first practiced.

There is a row of 10 round projections on each side of the pedestal, just above the door. In Hunt's original plan, each of these would have been decorated with the shield of one of the United States (adding the shield of the federal District of Columbia would have brought the total up to 40). These decorations were never added, probably due to a lack of funding.

The door on each side of the pedestal is five feet wide and 13 feet high. Each side of the pedestal is 62 feet wide at the base, tapering to 39 feet, 4 inches at the top.

The pedestal's walls are 17.5 feet thick at the base, six feet thick at the top.

Before the first elevator was installed in 1909, the only way to reach the top of the pedestal was by climbing an iron staircase. The two-story hydraulic elevator pictured above was built for the statue's 1986 centennial. It was replaced in 2012 as part of a year-long, $27.5 million safety and accessibility upgrade. With the newest elevators, visitors in wheelchairs can finally reach the observation deck at the top of the pedestal.

Visitors who climb the pedestal stairs will see eight enormous beams. Set into the concrete walls, they form two squares: one just below the top of the pedestal, the other 26 feet above its base. To stabilize the statue in heavy winds, military engineer Charles P. Stone anchored Eiffel's armature to both sets of beams.

Stone also designed the pedestal's foundation: a square pyramid of concrete, 62 feet high and 91 feet wide at its base. Anchored to bedrock 20 feet underground, the pedestal is solid but for a 10-foot shaft for stairs and an elevator.

The New Colossus (1883) by Emma Lazarus

Not like the brazen giant of Greek fame,
With conquering limbs astride from land to land;
Here at our sea-washed, sunset gates shall stand
A mighty woman with a torch, whose flame
Is the imprisoned lightning, and her name
Mother of Exiles. From her beacon-hand
Glows world-wide welcome; her mild eyes command
The air-bridged harbor that twin cities frame.
"Keep, ancient lands, your storied pomp!" cries she
With silent lips. "Give me your tired, your poor,
Your huddled masses yearning to breathe free,
The wretched refuse of your teeming shore.
Send these, the homeless, tempest-tossed to me,
I lift my lamp beside the golden door!"

In December, 1883, the National Academy of Design sponsored an Art Loan Exhibition to raise money for Liberty's pedestal. The works on display ranged from paintings, drawings, and prints to stained glass, old books and coins, and such curiosities as a padlock from the Bastille. Writers such as Mark Twain and Walt Whitman donated original manuscripts to be sold at auction.

The manuscript that received the highest bid— $1500—almost didn't get written. When the Academy asked poet and essayist Emma Lazarus to write a poem about the Statue of Liberty for the Exhibition catalog, she turned them down. What was there to say about a statue?

She soon reconsidered. Born into a Jewish family that settled in New York before the Revolution, Emma Lazarus devoted much of her time and effort to Jewish causes, here and abroad. After witnessing the persecution of Jews during a tour of Europe, she began teaching at a school for Jewish immigrants and speaking and writing about the need for a Jewish homeland. She wrote *The New Colossus* for the Art Loan catalog after realizing the Statue of Liberty would be the first thing future immigrants saw when their ships entered New York Harbor.

Emma Lazarus died in 1888, at the age of 37, long before the closing lines of her sonnet became almost as familiar as the statue they celebrated. The *New York Times* and the *New York World* reprinted the poem in 1886 for the statue's dedication, and it was included in an 1888 collection of her writings. In

1903, *The New Colossus* was cast in bronze and displayed at the Statue of Liberty.

Did you know?

Irving Berlin was a Russian Jew who arrived in New York with his family in 1893, when he was just five years old. He set the last lines of *The New Colossus* to music in 1949, as *Give Me Your Tired, Your Poor*. The song appeared in his Broadway musical *Miss Liberty*, which ran for 308 performances in 1949–50. The show told the story of a fictional search for the model that inspired the Statue of Liberty.

The Immigrants (1973) by Luis Sanguino
Dedicated in Battery Park on May 4, 1983, the monument includes four figures, representing immigrants from around the world: a worker, a priest, a freed African-American slave, and an Eastern European Jew.

Liberty Enlightening the World (1885) by Currier and Ives. The statue actually faces east, not south as in this picture.

Chapter Six

Liberty Enlightening the World

When Liberty was being restored for her 1986 centennial, she was surrounded by a 250-foot high, 300-ton aluminum scaffold. Attached to the concrete and granite pedestal, no part of the scaffold touched the statue's copper skin.

No scaffolding touched her in the summer and fall of 1886, either—because none was used. The workers who riveted the hundreds of copper pieces to Eiffel's armature had only the ironwork itself to stand on. Fortunately, no one died during the construction.

The Statue of Liberty was dedicated on October 28, 1886. Despite cold winds and rain, 20,000 men marched in the morning parade from 57th Street to the Battery. A million spectators lined the five-mile route, and hundreds of ships and boats clogged New York Harbor. Liberty's face was covered by a large sheet of canvas, painted to resemble a French flag.

The ceremonies on Bedloe's Island began with a prayer by historian and theologian Richard Storrs, pastor of Brooklyn's Church of the Pilgrims. He was followed by Ferdinand de Lesseps, president of the French-American Union, and William Evarts, chairman of the American Committee.

Kevin Woyce

Dedication of the Statue of Liberty on October 28, 1886. Taken aboard the steamship *Patrol*, this is the only known photograph of the day's events.

Mistaking a pause in Evarts' speech for the long-awaited signal to "unveil" the statue, Bartholdi cut the ropes holding the giant flag a few minutes early. Cheers, steam whistles, and naval salutes filled the harbor for the next fifteen minutes.

When the noise finally subsided, President Grover Cleveland formally accepted the statue as a gift from the people of France. "We will not forget," he told the crowd, "that Liberty has here made her home."

The evening's fireworks were postponed, due to the rainy weather.

When he presented the Statue of Liberty to the United States, Ferdinand de Lesseps described her as "a grand beacon raised in the midst of the waves at the threshold of free America." He was not just being poetic. Bartholdi always intended Liberty to serve as a lighthouse, and Congress placed the United States Lighthouse Board in charge of her illumination and maintenance.

Liberty became the nation's first electrified lighthouse on November 1, 1886. At sundown, her keeper switched on the nine electric arc lamps inside her torch flame, along with five others spaced around the points of Fort Wood.

The Lighthouse Board's decision to place the lights inside the flame was made during the final months of the statue's construction. Bartholdi's plan had been to put the lights inside the head, so they would shine through the crown's 25 windows. To accommodate the Lighthouse Board, he approved a plan to cut two rows of round windows in the thin copper skin of the flame.

Though the light was designed to be seen up to 24 miles away, sailors often complained about its dimness. (Because the flame is 300 feet from the water, fogs sometimes hid it completely.) Bartholdi himself, returning to the United States in 1893 for the Chicago World's Fair, compared it to a glowworm.

By then, the bottom row of windows had been replaced with a wide band of colored glass. The Lighthouse Board tried several times during the next decade to brighten the light. Nothing worked, and in

1902, Liberty was removed from the nation's roster of active lighthouses. She was maintained by the Army until 1933, when the National Park Service took over.

Sculptor Gutzon Borglum made the last major changes to Liberty's original flame in 1916. (Borglum is best known for carving the faces of presidents George Washington, Thomas Jefferson, Abraham Lincoln, and Theodore Roosevelt on Mount Rushmore. He worked on the monument from 1927 until his death in 1941. The work was completed the following year by his son, Lincoln.) He trimmed the flame's remaining copper to little more than a mesh framing 250 pieces of amber-colored glass.

After so many changes, the flame leaked badly, allowing rainwater to rust the ironwork supporting the right arm. (Many believe this is why only maintenance workers are allowed to climb to the torch. But it was actually closed to visitors in 1916, because of the difficulty of climbing the ladders inside the 47-foot arm.)

The face on Mount Rushmore is not Borglum's only sculpture of Abraham Lincoln. He carved a marble head of the 16th president for the Capitol Rotunda in 1908. Three years later, his bronze sculpture of Lincoln seated on a bench was dedicated in front of the Essex County Courthouse in Newark, New Jersey.

Liberty's flame was replaced in 1986. The original is displayed in the museum.

The "Light of Freedom" shines from Liberty's crown in seven rays, up to nine feet long. Although Bartholdi never explained the significance of the crown, many people believe the rays represent the world's seven continents, making Liberty a universal symbol of freedom. (Seven is also the traditional number of the world's seas, and of the Wonders of the Ancient World.)

Historian Yasmin Khan suggested another interpretation in her 2010 book Enlightening the World: The Creation of the Statue of Liberty. Recalling Laboulaye's fascination with early American history, Khan noticed the resemblance between Liberty's crown and the sun painted on the back of the armchair George Washington used during the 1787 Constitutional Convention.

Laboulaye's hero, Benjamin Franklin, attended every session of the Convention, although he was in his 80s and in failing health. Whenever he had comments or suggestions to make, he wrote them for other delegates to read.

James Madison wrote that on the last day of the convention, Franklin said he had often wondered about the sun on Washington's chair. "Now," the old statesman concluded, "I have the happiness to know that it is a rising and not a setting sun."

Bartholdi intended the 25 windows in Liberty's crown to shine like gemstones when she was used as a lighthouse.

Kevin Woyce

It was not just the dimness of the light in the flame that disappointed Bartholdi when he visited the statue in 1893. He also saw that, after only seven years in New York Harbor, patches of Liberty's copper skin were beginning to turn a pale green.

The color change was caused by oxidation, a chemical reaction between copper and air which creates a thin layer of *verdigris* on the outside of the copper. The change occurs more quickly when the air is humid or salty.

Verdigris does not harm the copper. Instead, it forms a protective coating, or "patina," on the outside of the metal, which prevents further corrosion.

Bartholdi's concern was that the dull green patina would not reflect light as well as the unblemished copper. Perhaps half-joking, he suggested to Congress that the entire statue should be covered with gold leaf. After rejecting this proposal as too expensive, Congress debated the cost and difficulty of painting the statue white. (Thankfully, they decided this would also be too expensive.)

During the Statue's 1980s restoration, small sections of the copper skin that had cracked or corroded needed to be replaced. At Bell Labs in Murray Hill, New Jersey, engineers studying the corrosion discovered that the verdigris matched that on the copper roof of their auditorium. Bell Labs donated part of the roof for repairs; in return, they received damaged copper from the statue for further studies.

Liberty turned green over a period of 20 years. After analyzing the patina, scientists at Bell Labs discovered a way to create an identical coating in just three weeks.

Did you know?

Liberty's original torch was removed on July 4, 1984. On January 1, 1985, it led the Tournament of Roses parade in Pasadena, sharing a float with 20,000 roses; a picture of Liberty's face made entirely of flowers; and Miss America 1984, Deborah Wolfe.

Covering the new flame with 980 small squares of 24K gold leaf took three weeks. (All of the gold used in the restoration was donated.)

The *International Herald Tribune* gave the city of Paris a gilded copper copy of the statue's flame in 1989. Called "The Flame of Liberty", it stands on a black marble pedestal in an intersection above the exit to the Pont de l'Alma Tunnel. Many tourists have mistaken the Flame for a monument to Princess Diana, who died in the tunnel in 1997.

Visitors can see two full-sized reproductions at the museum on Liberty Island. Made of new copper, and protected from the harbor air, they suggest what the statue looked like before she turned green.

Above: Liberty's left foot. Look closely, and you can see that it is made of several pieces of copper riveted together.

Page 76: Bartholdi said that Liberty's face was modeled after his mother, Charlotte. The eyes are 2.5 feet wide, the nose is four feet long, and the mouth is three feet wide.

Castle Clinton National Monument (1811) Battery Park, NY.

Chapter Seven

Castle Garden

By the 1850s, about 70% of all the immigrants coming to the United States were landing in New York City. Because there would not be a Federal Bureau of Immigration until 1890, each state was responsible for admitting and documenting the immigrants who reached its shores. In most places, New York included, their arrival was noted at whichever pier their ship tied up to.

With 150,000 immigrants coming ashore every year, at piers all around the city, New York needed a better system.

New York State created a Board of Emigration Commissioners in 1847. The following year, the Commissioners established the Verplanck State Emigrant Hospital on Ward's Island in the East River. This was soon joined by a refuge for women and children; a barracks for single men; and a smallpox hospital on nearby Blackwell's Island.

Next, the Commissioners decided that all immigrants arriving in New York should land at the same location. Despite loud protests from neighboring landowners, they decided this should be an old fort at the southern tip of Manhattan, in what is now Battery Park.

Antique cannon, inside Castle Clinton National Monument. Historical displays line the inside of the sandstone wall.

Castle Clinton was built between 1807 and 1811 as the "West Battery;" along with the "East Battery"— Castle Williams on Governor's Island—it was intended to protect southern Manhattan. (The name was changed to Castle Clinton in 1815, to honor New York's first governor, George Clinton). Armed with 28 guns, which were never fired except for target practice, the round sandstone fort originally stood more than 200 feet offshore, in 35 feet of water. A wooden causeway and drawbridge provided access until the 1850s, when the city enlarged Battery Park with landfill.

The Army gave the fort to New York in 1821. Three years later, a group of restaurant operators

80

leased it for 30 years. Changing the name to Castle Garden, they decorated the interior with panoramas and statuary, flowers, shrubs, and eventually a large fountain. By the mid-1840s, they had added a second story and a roof, transforming the fort into a 6,000 seat opera house. Promoted by P.T. Barnum, "Swedish Nightingale" Jenny Lind began her American tour here, with 11 sold-out shows in September, 1850.

New York did not renew the lease in 1854, and the Board of Emigration Commissioners claimed the building the following May. On August 3, 1855, they reopened the fort as the Castle Garden Emigrant Landing Depot. Over the next 35 years, more than eight million immigrants passed through its gate.

Everything immigrants needed to begin their new lives was located in or around the fort, from washrooms and restaurants to railroad agents, a currency exchange, and an employment office. The staff of 100 included doctors, record clerks, and interpreters fluent in every major European language.

By the 1880s, the flood of immigrants was more than the old fort or its staff could handle. Of the more than five million immigrants who came to the United States between 1880 and 1890, almost four million landed at Castle Garden. Some days, thousands of people landed, and had to wait for hours on wooden benches for their interviews and examinations.

There were other problems as well: corruption, scandals, and the dangers immigrants faced in the city. When they left the fort, many newcomers fell prey to swindlers, pickpockets, or worse.

Early postcard view of Castle Garden during its years as the New York City Aquarium, "which has the finest collection of living fish ever displayed."

The Supreme Court ruled in 1875 that regulating immigration was a federal responsibility. Congress passed several immigration laws in the 1880s, and Castle Garden welcomed its last immigrants on April 18, 1890. For the next year and a half, the new Federal Bureau of Immigration would receive immigrants at the nearby "Barge Office."

In 1896, Castle Garden became the New York City Aquarium. It remained a popular attraction until 1940, when Parks Commissioner Robert Moses ordered it demolished. In the late 1930s, he had wanted to build ramps across Battery Park for a proposed Brooklyn-Battery Bridge. After the bridge plan was defeated in 1939, thanks to a timely plea from first lady Eleanor Roosevelt, Moses warned that the walls of the old fort would be dangerously undermined if a tunnel was built instead. To prepare for the demolition, all of the aquarium's fish and sea creatures were moved to the Bronx Zoo.

By the time Castle Clinton was declared a National Monument in 1946, only the 1811 sandstone walls remained standing.

The Brooklyn-Battery Tunnel, in planning since 1929, opened on May 25, 1950. In 1957, the city opened a new aquarium on the Coney Island boardwalk. Castle Clinton was finally restored and reopened to the public in 1975. Ticket booths for Circle Line ferries to the Statue of Liberty were added in 1986.

Chapter Eight

Ellis Island

The Federal Bureau of Immigration opened its Ellis Island station on January 1, 1892. To celebrate, Superintendent John Weber gave the first immigrant ashore—15-year-old Annie Moore—a $10 gold coin, with which to start her new life in the United States (according to legend, she landed on her birthday).

Ellis was not the Bureau's first, or even second, choice. But the Army would not allow immigrants to land on Governor's Island, and plans to build the station on Bedloe's Island were loudly denounced by both Joseph Pulitzer and Frederic Bartholdi (the sculptor called the "monstrous plan" a "desecration").

That left Ellis. The Army had shut down Battery Gibson in the early 1860s. By the end of the decade the Navy, which had begun storing ammunition at the fort in 1835, had 3,000 barrels of powder on the island. Fearing the results of an accident or a lightning strike, the citizens of nearby Jersey City demanded they be removed. Although their complaints were ignored time and again, they finally got their wish in April of 1890, when the Navy began vacating the island for the Bureau of Immigration.

Kevin Woyce

The Bureau doubled the size of the island—from three acres to six—with landfill, and then built a $500,000 wooden station, 400 feet long and 150 feet wide. With its peaked slate roof and a square tower at each corner, the building was visible throughout the harbor. Newspaper reporters compared it to the giant hotels at nearby beach resorts.

The station burned on June 14, 1897. Because the fire started just after midnight, the station was empty and there were no casualties. But the building was completely destroyed, along with many of the paper records from Castle Garden.

After three and a half years of screening immigrants at Battery Park's crowded Barge Office, the Bureau opened a new, fireproof Ellis Island station on December 17, 1900. Four ships arrived that day, bringing a total of 2,251 immigrants.

Architects William Boring and Edward Tilton designed the new station to accommodate up to half a million immigrants each year. By 1907, more than a million were arriving. Ships sometimes had to wait a day or more in the harbor before landing. On the station's busiest day ever—April 17, 1907—a total of 11,745 immigrants passed through the vaulted Registry Hall. Doctors had just two minutes a person to decide who was healthy enough to enter the country, who needed to be hospitalized, and who should be refused entry. (One way doctors judged immigrants' fitness was by watching them climb the stairs to the Registry Hall.)

The Registry Hall is *189 feet long and 102 feet wide,
with a 60-foot high vaulted ceiling containing more
than 28,000 tiles. The original stone ceiling collapsed
on the night of July 30, 1916, when the munitions
stored on nearby Black Tom Island exploded. The
explosion is believed to have been triggered by
German saboteurs, aiming to keep the powder and
shells out of Allied hands. Though there were no
deaths or serious injuries on Ellis, the island was
evacuated until the fire was extinguished.*

Ellis Island Ferry Building (1935, restored 2007).

If they passed their inspections, immigrants boarded ferries bound for New York or for the railroad terminals on the Jersey City waterfront. Those needing medical attention were admitted to one of the island's hospitals; others waited for legal decisions in dormitories or barracks. Some years, as many as 2% of arriving immigrants were turned away. In their memories, and the memories of those who knew them, Ellis remained "The Island of Tears."

Immigration slowed during the First World War, when German U-Boats terrorized the Atlantic. 878,000 people landed at Ellis Island in 1914. Four years later, the number was just 28,867.

The numbers began rising again after the fighting ended in 1918, but never returned to prewar levels.

Congress had passed a law in 1917 requiring all prospective immigrants to pass a literacy test. This was followed in the 1920s by a series of increasingly restrictive "Quota Laws," limiting the number of immigrants who would be accepted each year from each country. (In 1921, the percentages were based on the number of people from each country who were living here in 1910. Three years later, the basis year was changed to 1890). Congress also steadily lowered the total number of immigrants who would be admitted each year. More than half a million people arrived in 1921. By 1929, only 150,000 were allowed to land. During the Great Depression of the 1930s, more people actually left the United States through Ellis Island than arrived.

Eventually, all immigrants were required to pass inspections and to receive visas at U.S. Consular Offices overseas. Only those needing medical attention, or awaiting the decision of a Board of Inquiry, landed at Ellis Island. During WWII, the Coast Guard occupied the island. Afterwards, it was used mostly as a detention center for those awaiting deportation.

The government closed the station in November, 1954 and offered island and its 35 buildings for sale as "surplus property." Over the next decade, there was talk of using Ellis Island as a university, a hospital, housing, a luxury resort, or a prison. Architect Frank Lloyd Wright suggested tearing down the abandoned buildings and replacing them with a "perfect city of tomorrow."

Kevin Woyce

Ellis Island, photographed from the top of Liberty's pedestal, with the towers of waterfront Jersey City in the background.

No buyers appeared, so on May 11, 1965, President Lyndon Johnson made Ellis Island part of the Statue of Liberty National Monument. The following year, architect Phillip Johnson submitted plans for a monumental wall, engraved with the names of the 16 million immigrants who landed on the island. Instead of restoring the empty buildings, already scarred by weather and vandalism, he suggested turning them into "instant ruins" by removing their roofs. (Neither part of his plan was adopted.)

President Calvin Coolidge had declared the Statue of Liberty a national monument in 1924.

In 1976, National Park Service personnel began walking 50,000 visitors a year through the island's ruined main building. The tours continued until 1984, when the building was closed for restoration.

Working with the Statue of Liberty–Ellis Island Foundation, the National Park Service transformed the sprawling ruin into the Ellis Island Immigration Museum. Open since 1990, the museum includes historical exhibits and theaters; an "American Immigrant Wall of Honor," inscribed with more than 700,000 names; and a family research center, with information on more than 25 million immigrants.

The nonprofit "Save Ellis Island" began working with the National Park Service in 1999 to restore the rest of the island's historic buildings. After removing all the vegetation that had grown up around, and even through, many of the buildings, they repaired leaking roofs, closed up broken windows, and installed firefighting and security equipment. By April, 2007, they had finished restoring the 1935 Ferry Building.

Kevin Woyce
Did you know?

For 50 years (1904-54), immigrants bound for New York rode the ferry *Ellis Island* to Manhattan. During the island's busiest years, she ran 18 hours a day. But when the station closed in 1955, the *Ellis Island* was abandoned at her dock, where she sank in 1968. Often visible at low tide, her remains were finally removed as a navigation hazard in 2009.

Fiorello LaGuardia was mayor of New York from 1934 to 1945. Many years earlier, he worked as an Ellis Island interpreter. Besides English, La Guardia spoke German, Italian, Hebrew, Yiddish, Hungarian, and Croatian.

Ellis Island architect Edward Tilton designed nearly 100 public libraries. Many of these were funded by Andrew Carnegie, founder of the United States Steel Corporation. Born in Scotland in 1835, Carnegie came to the United States with his parents when he was 13. After building one of the world's largest fortunes, he turned to philanthropy; between 1883 and 1929, he donated money for the establishment of 2,509 libraries, including 1,689 in the United States.

Ellis Island, photographed from Manhattan's Battery Park.

Statue Cruises ferry *Miss Ellis Island* at Liberty State Park in Jersey City, NJ.

Chapter Nine

Liberty State Park

For Morris Pesin, the opening of Liberty State Park on June 14, 1976 was a dream that took 19 years to come true. He had visited the Statue of Liberty with his wife and children in the summer of 1957. Because of traffic, the trip from Jersey City took three hours. When they arrived, Pesin noticed how close Liberty Island was to his hometown. He also wished the statue had a better backdrop than the rotting docks and abandoned factories on the old industrial waterfront.

But Pesin was not just an idle dreamer. All his life, he had worked for causes he believed in. As a lawyer, he had fought to end racial segregation and to protect religious freedom.

Now he began a campaign to transform the Jersey City waterfront. On June 13, 1958, reporters watched him row to Liberty Island in a rented canoe.

This trip took eight minutes.

"We have at our doorstep America's greatest shrine," Pesin said, "and we have failed to realize its potential." He recommended cleaning up the depressed waterfront and building a pedestrian bridge to Liberty Island.

The bridge was never built. But Pesin gathered a group of activists and believers, and in August of 1965, Jersey City deeded 165 acres to the state for a park. The New Jersey Department of Environmental Protection began buying additional land in the early 1970s. Slowly, the factories and warehouses were razed, the railroad tracks pulled up, and the piers rebuilt or demolished.

The creation of Liberty State Park is an ongoing process. Today there are walking trails, ball fields and picnic groves; an interpretive center, a marina, and the Liberty Science Center. In areas still closed to the public, the NJDEP is working with the nonprofit Friends of Liberty State Park to restore wetlands and natural areas long covered with rail yards and factories. The Friends have also worked since 1988 to block the commercialization of the park, including efforts to build a golf course, a waterpark, and condominiums.

A waterfront monument in the park's northeastern corner honors the New Jersey victims of the September 11, 2001 terrorist attacks. Dedicated September 10, 2011, *Empty Sky* is two stainless steel walls, each 30 feet high and 200 feet long. Inscribed with 746 names, the walls frame visitors' views of the former site of the Twin Towers.

Used as a staging ground for rescue and relief efforts following the towers' collapse, Liberty State Park also includes a 750-tree Grove of Remembrance.

One World Trade Center's spire reaches 1776 feet, making it the United States' tallest building.

Kevin Woyce

Much of Liberty State Park is built on land created by New Jersey's 19th century canal and railroad companies. The Morris Canal Company arrived first, completing an 11-mile extension from Newark to Jersey City in 1836. Freight was unloaded at a riverfront terminal, and two wide basins allowed the 70-ton, 87-foot canal boats to turn around. The basins were abandoned in the 1920s, after the canal was closed and drained. By the 1950s, they were filled with garbage and abandoned boats. Today, they are part of the picturesque waterway along the park's northern edge.

By the early 1860s, the Central Railroad of New Jersey had claimed most of the Jersey City waterfront through a series of mergers and lawsuits. After extending its property 4,000 feet into the Hudson with landfill—mostly garbage towed over on barges from New York—the CRRNJ built its first riverfront terminal in 1864. This was replaced in 1886 with the present three-story, red brick terminal.

The Lehigh Valley Railroad, which bought control of the Morris Canal in the 1870s, built its riverfront terminal in what is now the southern part of Liberty State Park. By the 1880s, its mile-long pier completely covered Black Tom Island. Today, the site of the 1916 munitions explosion is marked with a plaque and a circle of American flags. No other trace of the railroad remains in the park.

So many Ellis Island immigrants passed through the 1886 Central Railroad of New Jersey Terminal that the building became known as the "Gateway to the West." (The CRRNJ even added the Statue of Liberty to its logo.) Closed since 1967, the terminal was fully restored in 2005, and how houses historical exhibits and ticket counters for the Statue of Liberty / Ellis Island ferries. The train shed behind the building, covering 20 tracks and 300,000 square feet, remains closed to visitors.

Kevin Woyce

Did you know?

President Reagan presented Morris Pesin with a Volunteer Action Award in 1985, recognizing the many years he devoted to Liberty State Park. Since Pesin's death in 1992, his son Sam has guided the efforts of the Friends of Liberty State Park.

The park's 1.3-mile riverfront trail, called "Liberty Walk," is part of a proposed Hudson River Walkway, stretching more than 18 miles from the Bayonne Bridge to the George Washington Bridge. (The total length of the trail, including detours around canal basins and other obstacles, will be almost 40 miles.) Though the trail has been under construction since the 1980s, so much of the riverfront is privately owned that many gaps remain. Whenever riverfront properties are redeveloped, their owners are required to set aside a 30-foot path for the trail.

The Statue of Liberty and Ellis Island, photographed from Liberty State Park. The bridge connecting the park to Ellis Island is not open to visitors.

One of the two "Centennial Doors" designed by sculptor Jordan Steckel and installed at Fort Wood's entrance in 1986.

Chapter Ten

Second Century

President Ronald Reagan announced the formation of the Statue of Liberty—Ellis Island Foundation on May 18, 1982. Helmed by Chrysler chairman Lee Iacocca, the organization raised nearly half a billion dollars to restore both monuments for their centennials. Like the French-American Union and the American Committee that built the statue and her pedestal, the Foundation would rely entirely on private donors, ranging from schoolchildren to international corporations.

After nearly a century in the harbor, Liberty was showing her age. Her torch leaked. Her iron framework was badly corroded. Shrapnel from the 1916 Black Tom explosion had punctured the copper skin of her right arm.

Maintenance had been ongoing. Her lighting system had been updated several times since the Lighthouse Service left in 1902. The Works Progress Administration of the 1930s replaced the pedestal's cast iron stairs with reinforced concrete, and rebuilt the iron supports in the crown's rays. The National Park Service added a heating system in 1949, and built a museum around the base of the pedestal in the 1970s.

Still, Liberty needed a complete renovation.

Engineers traced some of the worst problems back to the 1880s. Parts of the copper skin arrived on Bedloe's Island already misshapen, damaged during packing or shipping. Worse, Eiffel's armature had been incorrectly assembled, misplacing Liberty's head almost two feet off center. By the 1980s, one of the rays on the crown had punctured her right arm.

Galvanic corrosion, caused by contact between two different metals, turned out to be one of the biggest problems. When the statue was built, hundreds of iron "ribs" were attached to the inside of the copper skin, to hold it rigid. The metals were separated by strips of asbestos and layers of shellac. But Liberty is never still. The skin and the framework were designed to flex in the wind, so over the years, the insulation wore away. As the iron deteriorated, hundreds of rivets popped loose, opening gaps in the skin for the rain to pour through.

Workers made stainless steel duplicates of every rib and all the iron bars linking them to the central pylon. To keep from stressing the century-old copper, the ironwork had to be removed and replaced one piece at a time. For insulation, all the new pieces were coated with Teflon.

Fort Wood's "Centennial Doors" are decorated with 10 sculpted panels (five on each door), describing Liberty's construction and renovation.

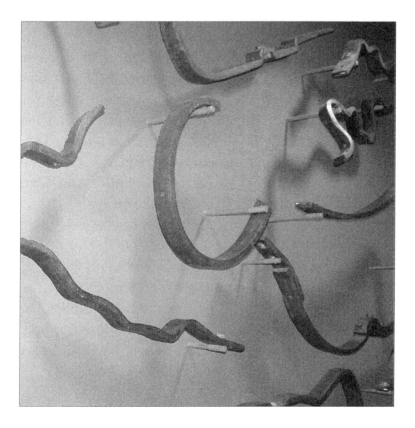

Iron bands removed from the statue during her 1980s renovation, displayed on a wall in the museum.

The Statue's museum was built in the 1970s, to house exhibits relating to immigration. The modern "Statue of Liberty Exhibit" was installed in 1986, after the National Park Service began restoring the main building on Ellis Island.

"We are the keepers of the flame of liberty," President Reagan told television viewers on July 3, 1986, the start of "Liberty Weekend." From Governor's Island, he activated the statue's new lighting system, so that Liberty seemed to appear out of the darkness. (Three years earlier, magician David Copperfield had created the opposite illusion on his television special *Vanishing the Statue of Liberty*.) On the morning of July 5, Nancy Reagan reopened the statue and led 100 French and American schoolchildren up the 354 steps to the crown.

New York's mayor, Edward Koch, described Liberty Weekend as "the Party of the Century" and said, "I invited the whole world." Highlights included performances by top stars; patriotic concerts by the Boston Pops and the New York Philharmonic; the world's largest fireworks display; and Operation Sail, featuring 33 tall ships from 14 nations. There was also a "Great Blimp Race" along the Hudson River.

The Statue of Liberty has been a popular tourist attraction since just after her dedication, when the American Committee launched the first ferry service from Battery Park. In 1890, she had 88,000 visitors. By the 1950s, half a million people were visiting every year. The number topped a million for the first time in 1964. And in 1987, the year after the Statue's renovation, Circle Line ferries brought more than three million tourists to Liberty Island.

The monument was closed following the 9/11 terrorist attacks. Though visitors were allowed back on the island in December, 2001, the pedestal remained closed until August, 2004. Since then, only 3,000 people have been admitted to the museum and pedestal each day. Because the island receives up to 15,000 visitors daily, the National Park Service recommends buying tickets in advance (at statuecruises.com).

The statue itself remained closed until June, 2009. For the next two years, the National Park Service allowed just 30 people every hour to climb to the crown; tickets sold out six months in advance.

Beginning October 29, 2011, Liberty was closed for a year-long renovation. All of the stairs and elevators were improved or replaced, and a three-person "rescue elevator" was installed inside the statue, alongside the spiral stairs.

Reopening ceremonies were held on October 28, 2012. The following day, Hurricane Sandy flooded Liberty Island's generators and badly damaged its seawall, docks, and walking paths. In the spring of 2013, the National Park Service announced that the island would be reopened to the public on July 4.

"This statue will remain ... it will stand there unshaken in the midst of the winds which will roar around its head and the waves which will shatter their fury at its feet."

—Edouard de Laboulaye, 1876

Kevin Woyce

Bibliography

Banks, Edgar. The Seven Wonders of the Ancient World. New York: G.P. Putnam's Sons, 1916.

Bartholdi, Frederic. The Statue of Liberty Enlightening the World Described by the Sculptor. New York: North American Review, 1885.

Bigelow, John. Some Recollections of the Late Edouard Laboulaye. New York: G.P. Putnam's Sons, 1889.

Burroughs, Tom. "Statue of Liberty." ChemMatters, April 1985.

Chandler, Arthur. "Empire of Autumn: The Paris Exposition Universelle of 1867." World's Fair Volume VI, Number 3 (1986).

Khan, Yasmin. Enlightening the World: The Creation of the Statue of Liberty. Ithaca: Cornell University Press, 2010.

Moreno, Barry. The Statue of Liberty Encyclopedia. New York: Simon & Schuster, 2000.

Novotny, Ann. Strangers at the Door: Ellis Island, Castle Garden, and the Great Migration to America. Riverside: The Chatham Press, Inc., 1971.

Pitkin, Thomas. Keepers of the Gate: A History of Ellis Island. New York: New York University Press, 1975.

Stengel, Richard. "The Party of the Century." Time. July 7, 1986.

Weinbaum, Paul. Statue of Liberty: Heritage of America. Las Vegas: KC Publications, 1979.

Woyce, Kevin. New Jersey State Parks: History & Facts. Lyndhurst: Kevin Woyce, 2011.

About the Author

Kevin Woyce is an author, photographer, and lecturer specializing in New Jersey and New York regional history. A lifelong resident of the Garden State, he grew up in East Rutherford, the eldest of 15 siblings. He now lives in Lyndhurst with his wife, Carin.

Website: KevinWoyce.com

Facebook: Kevin Woyce Author

Books by Kevin Woyce:

Lighthouses: Connecticut & Block Island

Lighthouses U.S.A. – Photographs by Kevin Woyce

Bridges – Photographs by Kevin Woyce

Niagara: The Falls and the River

Jersey Shore History & Facts

Made in the USA
Middletown, DE
21 June 2019